TABLE OF CONTENTS

CHAPTER 1: INTRODUCTION

This paper investigates the problem of how United States Department of Defense (DoD) force planners should organize the U.S. military, specifically the ground combat elements of the Army and Marine Corps, to meet near-to-mid term security challenges in a fiscally sustainable way. The post-Cold War force structure requires more to be spent on defense than two generations ago; yet is ill-suited to manage the challenges of the twenty-first century strategic environment. In short, the U.S. military has become fiscally unsustainable while the world has become less secure. As such, a drawdown of U.S. military force structure is on the horizon. The question that remains is how to accomplish this drawdown without "hollowing out" the military that remains behind. The thesis of this paper is that twentieth-century history provides recommendations to meet the challenges of the strategic environment while preventing another hollowing out of U.S. conventional combat capabilities. This paper examines history to glean lessons learned and provide policy, personnel, training and material recommendations for current force planners to posture the ground combat elements of the U.S. military to meet its mission requirements during the 2015 – 2020 period.

Defining the Problem

Twentieth-century U.S. military history has shown that as combat missions end or transition to stabilization and/or advisory roles, the United States will look to drawdown the size of the U.S. military in an effort to shrink defense budgets. The challenge with the impending military drawdown is the maintenance of sufficient capability within the

Armed Forces so that they are not found "hollow" when called upon to defend the nation. An historical case study of twentieth-century post-war periods reveals that likely challenges for the future, in many ways, resemble the issues force planners have faced over the last one hundred years. The United States military experienced a number of drawdowns during the twentieth-century and, more often than not, it hollowed out the Armed Forces in the process of drawing them down.

The term "Hollow Force" gained favor in 1950 after the poor performance of Task Force SMITH on the Korean Peninsula in July of that year.[1] It was coined as a way of describing a military that, while robust on paper, was unable to accomplish its primary mission of fighting and winning the Nation's conventional wars. This hollowness, or lack of capability, has manifested itself, typically after periods of prolonged combat, in a number of ways: an inherently flawed, or unrealistic, security policy; acute manpower reductions that render units combat ineffective or eliminated altogether; deficiencies in the quantity and quality of material; or an inability to train properly to the unit's mission essential task list. For the purposes of this paper, the author will examine each of these areas, their interrelationships and the impact the paradigmatic thinking of the time had on the hollowing of military capability.

The problem facing force planners is essentially a non-linear risk management issue. The problem is a risk management issue because the vulnerability imposed by limited resources makes it impossible to eliminate risk. The current problem is exacerbated by "years of rising fiscal and trade deficits [that] will… necessitate hard choices in the years

---

[1] For a detailed discussion of Task Force SMITH, see Roy K. Flint, "Task Force Smith and the 24th Division: Delay and Withdrawal, 5-19 July 1950," in *America's First Battles 1776-1965,* ed. Charles E. Heller and William A. Stofft (Lawerence, KS: University Press of Kansas, 1986), 266-299.

ahead."[2] This means politicians are going to be forced to choose which vulnerabilities are addressed and where to accept risk. In essence, force planners are forced into a deliberate hollowing of some capabilities and develop courses of action to identify and mitigate those hazards that remain. The problem is further defined as non-linear because it is both an art and a science of weaving together the complexities of the strategic environment with the cause and effect of innumerable variables. This must be accomplished while simultaneously maintaining the strategic depth and flexibility to account for the uncertain domestic and international environments, which are typified by the idiosyncrasies of world leaders, economic trends, and cultural and historical differences. This combination of art and science is made more difficult today as the United States finds itself in an era of persistent fiscal constraint combined with continuing conflict.

Planners, therefore, must attain a balance between sufficient and ready forces within the fiscal constraints of declining defense budgets. To accomplish this, planners must focus on creating a force that is capable of adjusting to risk and surprise with minimum difficulty rather than building a force that eliminates it. The recommendations in Chapter Three provide solutions to this risk management problem by examining historical examples within the present context to create a balanced force capable of adapting to the challenges of the future.[3]

---

[2] U.S. President. *National Security Strategy.* (Washington, DC: May 2010), 9.

[3] U.S. Joint Forces Command, *The Joint Operating Environment 2008: Challenges and Implications for the Future Joint Forces* (Norfolk, VA: U.S. Joint Forces Command, 15 October 2008), 3.

CHAPTER 2: UNITED STATES GROUND FORCES IN 2010

In order to make recommendations on how to a hollow military force, planners must first understand the "implications of those issues that have greatest impact on force structure [to] develop force structure that most nearly meets national security objectives."[1] This chapter examines those implications to establish the point of departure for making recommendations by analyzing the current state of U.S. ground forces through policy, manpower, training, and material rubrics. Additionally, external factors influencing force planner decision making and the assumptions required to move forward with the analysis are established.

The U.S. Armed Forces today are likely the most capable military in the history of the world. The difference in the conventional capabilities possessed by the U.S. Army and Marine Corps and those of the next closest competitor is so wide that it is unlikely that the United States will be challenged in this arena for the foreseeable future. The same cannot be said, however, of U.S. irregular warfare capabilities. Despite nine years of fighting in Iraq and Afghanistan, U.S. ground forces have not yet achieved the level of mastery of this skill-set to dissuade would-be adversaries from extremism and insurgency as the means to achieve political objectives.

---

[1] Edward Stellini, "Force Structure Planning Considerations, Problems and Issues," *Air University Review* (May-June 1971), available at http://www.airpower.au.af.mil/airchronicles/aureview/1971/may-jun/Stellini.html (accessed 14 October 2010).

State of the Force Today

Policy - 2010 Quadrennial Defense Review (QDR)

The first step in assessing the near-to-mid term force structure is to examine current U.S. security policy, as this should codify the objectives. Only with a detailed understanding of national security objectives can force planners begin to develop the forces and mechanisms necessary to meet those objectives. The 2010 Quadrennial Defense Review (QDR) provides the DoD's mission requirements and policy guidance used in the formulation of recommendations in this paper.

Since the 2010 QDR explicitly links force planning with the priority objectives of the defense strategy, a review of that document is necessary to provide force planners with the capacity and capability desired in the future Armed Forces. The mission requirements dictated to the DoD in the QDR are Prevail in Today's War, Prevent and Deter War, Prepare to Defeat Adversaries and Succeed in a Wide Range of Contingencies, and Preserve and Enhance the All-Volunteer Force.[2] These mission requirements provide force planners with the priority objectives, or ends, for the determination of ways and means to be committed. However, they do not define the precedence among those priority objectives and appear to be a hedge against "all combinations of foreign powers."[3] These mission requirements and their implications provide the framework force planners will use in developing the 2015 to 2020 U.S. Armed Forces.

---

[2] U.S. Department of Defense, *Quadrennial Defense Review Report*. (Washington, DC: February 2010),v- vii.

[3] Ray S. Cline, *Washington Command Post: The Operations Division*. (Washington, DC: U.S. Army, Center of Military History, 1951), 36.

Prevail in Today's War

This objective is the central objective for the DoD for the foreseeable future.[4]
Today's War is understood to be a long-term, episodic, multi-front, multi-dimensional
conflict that will require the refinement and synchronization of kinetic and non-kinetic
capabilities that U.S. ground forces have developed over the last nine years of combat in
Iraq and Afghanistan. The implication of this mission requirement is that DoD must
remain capable of sustaining force applications activities across the spectrum of conflict
over the long term while continuing to develop the capacity to defeat the enemy using an
indirect approach.

Prevent and Deter War

Although the QDR does not specify which war DoD is to prevent and deter, it does
specify that the Department will assume "a broader and deeper range of prevent and deter
missions" than it has traditionally been tasked with.[5] In order to meet this broader and
deeper range of missions, the DoD must maintain capacity and capability across the
entire spectrum of conflict. Additionally, DoD must be able to assure strategic access
and freedom of action in areas vital to U.S. interests, maintain security conditions
favorable to the international order, and assist the U.S. government with consequence
management at home and abroad. To be effective, deterrence must be measured "on the
ability of a trained contingency force, but also on the potential of the strategic and
conventional forces available to a nation."[6] An important implication of this objective is

---

[4] U.S. Department of Defense, *National Defense Strategy*, (Washington, DC: June 2008), 7.

[5] U.S. DoD, *QDR*, vi.

[6] Charles E. Heller, "The New Military Strategy and its Impacts on the Reserve Components." (Master's thesis, U.S. Army War College, 1991), 30.

that the capabilities to be successful in preventing and deterring a conventional war with China are very different from those required to prevail in today's counterinsurgency wars in Iraq and Afghanistan.

Prepare to Defeat Adversaries in a Wide Range of Contingencies

Implied within this objective is the ability of the United States to have "sufficient combat power to prevail in contested forcible entry operations" against previously unexpected threats.[7] Although major conventional conflict would appear to be the exception over the near-to-mid term, history has shown that the United States ignores conventional war at its peril. The lethality of the modern battlefield demands that conventional conflicts are won quickly and that U.S. Armed Forces must remain "prepared to win the first battle of the next war."[8] Since the potential next war covers a wider range of threats than previous periods, the United States must have sufficient capability to respond to crises across the spectrum of conflict.

Preserve and Enhance the All-Volunteer Force

The primary consideration with this objective is the maintenance within the U.S. Armed Forces of sufficient force structure to attain deployment-to-dwell (DTD) ratios that are commensurate with an all-volunteer force. This ratio compares the amount of time that a service member spends operationally deployed with the amount of time spent at home and is the key determinant of operational tempo. For the Active Component, a one to three DTD ratio is ideal for allowing forces to reset and reconstitute the force.

---

[7] U.S. Department of Defense, *Force Application Functional Concept,* (Washington, DC: 5 March 2004), 10.

[8] FM 100-5 as quoted in John L. Romjue, From *Active Defense to AirLand Battle: The Development of Army Doctrine, 1973-1982.* (Fort Monroe, VA: Historical Office, U.S. Army Training and Doctrine Command, 1984), 6.

Department of Defense Instruction 1235.12, Accessing the Reserve Components directs that the Reserve Component maintain a deployment-to-dwell ratio of one to five.[9]

Manpower

Current manpower levels of U.S. ground combat forces are at an eighteen-year high and this relatively robust force size has been crucial to the recent operational successes in Iraq.[10] This historically high level is due to the addition of 65,000 active duty personnel in the Army and 27,000 personnel in the Marine Corps since 2007. These force levels, along with an increased reliance on an operational Reserve Component for additional manpower, have permitted most active duty forces to achieve a deployment-to-dwell ratio approaching one-to-three. This reduced operating tempo has allowed units to reconstitute forces upon redeployment and conduct pre-deployment training prior to deploying again.

Training

Although units have more time to train for deployment than just a few years ago, training in conventional warfare core competencies has suffered due to the nearly exclusive focus on training requirements for counterinsurgency operations in Iraq and Afghanistan and the associated high deployment rate. Particularly, combined arms skills across the Army and Marine Corps have eroded as units are being tasked with missions outside of their core competencies. This lack of core competency proficiency is a primary concern of both the Army Chief of Staff and the Commandant of the Marine Corps.

---

[9] U.S. Department of Defense, *Department of Defense Instruction 1235.12, Accessing the Reserve Components (RC)* (Washington, DC: February 4, 2010), 2.

[10] Data mined from U.S. Department of Defense Statistical Information Analysis Division, available at http://siadapp.dmdc.osd.mil/personnel/MILITARY/miltop.htm (accessed 7 April 2011).

Material

Both the Army and Marine Corps are in need of recapitalization of combat equipment after nine years of hard use in a combat zone. For example, the Army will need to revitalize its entire fleet of self-propelled 155mm howitzers between 2010 and 2021 due to the unusually high wear out rates associated with operations in Iraq and Afghanistan.[11] Funding for modernization efforts has fallen over the last ten years as procurement funds have been diverted to counterinsurgency specific material and operations. The modernization problem is growing especially acute since the "procurement holiday" of the 1990's only deferred the costs of needed investments.

Factors Influencing Force Structure Planning

Besides likely threat scenarios and budgetary considerations, a number of external factors influence the force structure decision-making process and must be considered during the force planning analysis. Among these are societal and political considerations, the economic conditions of the time, and the state of defense technology in the United States and around the world. In addition, defense planners have to examine the unintended consequences of their actions as well as wild-card scenarios. Each of these factors can have positive or negative impacts on the solutions that force planners ultimately implement.

Societal and political considerations have always played a major role in U.S. force structure decisions. For example, political and societal factors may make maintenance and upgrades to nuclear deterrence arsenals a hard sell. This in turn could place a greater

---

[11] Congressional Budget Office, *Long Term Implications of FY10 Defense Budget*, (Washington, DC: Congressional Budget Office, January 2010), 23.

burden on conventional forces to achieve a deterrent effect. The 1934 Nye Committee hearings are but one example where American war weariness has led the public and political leadership to confuse capabilities for war with its causes.[12] The period between the World Wars shows that once the move toward disarmament gains momentum, it can be impossible to stop. War Department attempts to test its mobilization plans in 1924 were cancelled because the program was politically opposed.[13] As late as 1939, President Roosevelt's efforts to increase the size of the Army were limited to only 17,000 personnel because of fears of political backlash to his calls for more forces.[14] Similarly, the Army was unable to recruit to its authorized endstrength after the Korean and Vietnam Wars because of, among other factors, anti-war sentiment.

Economic factors, good and bad, can distract the Nation from defense planning. The prosperity of the 1920's and 1990's created senses of euphoria that consumed the United States and made serious contemplation on national security issues an afterthought. Conversely, the economic hardships of the 1930's and concerns about rising budget deficits after World War II relegated defense expenditures to matters of little relative public importance. Specified and unspecified budget ceilings are often imposed upon force planners regardless of the visible threat signposts. Efforts to realize efficiency run the risk of using a strict cost-benefit analysis in instances where they are not actually relevant.

---

[12] C. Joseph Bernado and Eugene H. Bacon, Ph. D., *American Military Policy: Its Development Since 1775* (Harrisburg: The Telegraph Press, 1961), 401.

[13] Ibid., 387-388.

[14] Ibid., 407.

Technology is often seen as a cost effective substitute for manpower that has the added benefit of removing ground forces from the sharp end of war. In reality, "sophisticated machinery does not always prove superior to manpower" and in many cases merely creates a new requirement for manpower.[15] The demonstrated effectiveness of a suicide bomber and an improvised explosive device suggest that America's advanced technology may not yield an inherent advantage over an asymmetric enemy. Additionally, the proliferation of technology in many ways has compounded the national security dangers by expanding the range of threats that must be defended. For example, defending the U.S. homeland against a covert infiltration of a nuclear weapon is a potentially greater challenge than intercepting an incoming missile. Any realistic look at force structure requirements must recognize that any practical enemy will actively search for ways to negate U.S. technological advantage and should assume that they will be successful, at least on some levels, in doing so.

The cause and effect of known and unknown variables and the unintended consequences of action and inaction must also be considered. The 12 January 1950, Formosa Line radio address by Secretary of State Acheson was intended to describe the defensive perimeter of American interests in the western Pacific mostly for the domestic political audience; however, it was misinterpreted by the North Koreans as a green light for their invasion of South Korea.[16] Similarly, Al Qaida has repeatedly referred to the 1994 withdrawal of U.S. forces from Somalia after the battle for Mogadishu as an

---

[15] David W. Tarr, *American Security in the Nuclear Age* (New York: Macmillan Publishing Company, 1966), 69.

[16] Secretary of State Acheson's description of the Formosa line excluded the Korean Peninsula from the United States' defensive perimeter in the Pacific.

exploitable weakness. These unintended consequences must be thought of not only from the U.S. perspective, but also from that of potential adversaries.

Planners must also plan against wild-card scenarios when looking at the security environment. These events are unlikely occurrences that are difficult to forecast, but can have significant bearing on the strategic environment. The 2001 attack on the World Trade Center is a most recent example of a wild-card scenario that has had a dramatic impact on force structure decisions since that time.[17]

Assumptions

The following assumptions are used by the author in preparing recommendations for avoiding a hollow force. The key with these assumptions is that they must be continually assessed so that planners are able to identify and evaluate indicators that reveal whether they have been invalidated.

1. The Department of Defense will flatten the defense budget (from 2010 levels) by cutting seventy-eight billion dollars and reinvesting another 100 billion dollars in savings by 2015.[18] This level of cuts will translate into a reduction in active duty endstrength.

2. Combat forces in Iraq and Afghanistan have been redeployed to home station by 2015. Forward forces in both countries are there in a training and advisory role only.

---

[17] Wild-card scenarios are plausible futures that violate one of the assumptions that underlie the strategy. Their purpose is to allow planners to develop signposts that assumptions are being violated and to identify actions to prevent the occurrence from happening. Additionally, they provide the foundation for consequence management planning. In addition to examining threats, these scenarios must be examined from the friendly perspective.

[18] U.S. Secretary of Defense. *Statement on Department Budget and Efficiencies,* as delivered by Secretary of Defense Robert M. Gates (The Pentagon, January 06, 2011), transcript available at http://www.defense.gov/speeches/speech.aspx?speechid=1527 (accessed 10 Apr 11).

3. Withdrawal of forces from Iraq and Afghanistan will not mean an end to hostilities in the Long War.[19] The requirement for security and stability operations and counterinsurgency operations will remain high.

4. Budget constraints and U.S. global responsibilities present what Andre Beaufre describes in *An Introduction to Strategy* as an ends-means conundrum where the importance of the ends are out of balance with the ways and means. This conundrum dictates a combination of direct threat and indirect pressure to bring ends and means in balance.[20] In the context of the Long War, this implies attacking terrorists and their capacity to operate while simultaneously supporting efforts in the Muslim world that create an environment inhospitable to violent extremism and insurgency.

5. Reinstituting the draft of conscripted soldiers is not an option.

---

[19] For the purposes of this paper, the "Long War" is defined as the series of campaigns to defeat violent Islamic extremism and creating a global environment inhospitable to violent extremists and all who support them. It is seen as a generational conflict against a committed enemy with global aspirations that has publicly articulated a timeline of decades to achieve his objectives.

[20] Andre Beaufre, *An Introduction to Strategy*, trans. R.H. Barry (New York: Frederick A. Praeger, 1965), 26.

CHAPTER 3: RECOMMENDATIONS

Background

This chapter will present the reader with eight recommendations on solving the non-linear risk management problem of force planning. These recommendations are based on the current defense policy as stated in the QDR and an assessment of the strategic environment with an emphasis on the risks that rising budget deficits have on U.S. national security. They are centrally focused on rebalancing capabilities and reforming institutions to enable success in the likely wars of the future while preparing for a wide range of contingencies.[1] They are generally categorized into policy, personnel, training, and material recommendations, but the interrelationships of these prevent a neat classification of any recommendation into any single category. These recommendations are furthered examined from the perspective of mitigating the four risk categories described in the 2010 Quadrennial Defense Review (QDR).

The first area in which the Armed Forces can be found hollow is via the policy of the government at the time. The hierarchical relationship policy has over strategy means that policy decisions will influence every aspect of national security planning. Therefore, it is essential that policy accurately reflect the security environment to ensure the other components of force planning support national objectives. Additionally, policy must be sufficiently flexible to adapt to an ever-changing international environment. This is especially true in periods of drawing down military forces. Policy establishes the

---

[1] U.S. Department of Defense, *Quadrennial Defense Review Report*. (Washington, DC: February 2010), 89.

national security objectives, the priority of these objectives relative to one another, and the resource allocation to meet those objectives. Historically, it was either the lack of a clearly defined policy or a policy that did not accurately reflect the strategic environment that found the Armed Forces hollow on the eve of American first battles of the twentieth-century. Both of these shortcomings informed force structure decisions that ultimately placed the United States in a position where the forces that were available were not properly suited to fight the wars of the twentieth century. As an example, the Root reforms after the Spanish-American War and the National Defense Act of 1916 did much to professionalize the Army in the early twentieth century. However, even these revolutionary changes to the Army were insufficient to overcome the U.S. neutrality policy that ignored the realities of the current strategic environment. The U.S. Army that entered World War I was a largely constabulary force that could muster little more than 200,000 men with barely enough artillery and machine guns to support itself. As a result, the thrown-together 1st Expeditionary Division that sailed for France in June of 1917 was composed of about two-thirds raw recruits that had done little to prepare for the large scale planning and maneuvering of divisions.[2]

The policy recommendations put forth in this paper stem from the need to define the national interests and objectives of the Long War to inform the utilization of the different elements of national power. This, in turn, will establish a hierarchy of those objectives,

---

[2] U.S. Army Center of Military History, "American Military History, Volume 2, Chapter 1, The U.S. Army In World War 1," U.S. Army Center of Military History, http://www.history.army.mil/books/amh-v2/amh%20v2/chapter1.htm (accessed 7Apr 11), 9-19.

provide priorities for resource allocation, and inform the commitment of military forces required in prosecuting the Long War.[3]

As defense budgets decline, defense planners are going to be forced into making tough choices: do they sacrifice the size of the military in order to make room for modernization efforts or do they maintain the size of the current force and forgo training and modernization programs? The post-war periods of the twentieth-century demonstrate that personnel reductions provide defense planners and civilian leadership with the "easiest" of these tough choices. Currently, personnel costs account for approximately twenty percent of the total defense budget and therefore provide a politically saleable potential for significant savings if these accounts are reduced.[4] The foundation for the personnel recommendations in this paper originate from the policy recommendation of reducing the two major regional conflict (MRC) force with one structured around a single MRC, homeland security, peacetime engagement, forward presence and small scale contingency, and prosecution of the Long War through an indirect approach.

Perhaps the most critical area for the potential hollowing of the Armed Forces is in training. The conventional operations in Afghanistan and Iraq demonstrate that highly trained forces are able to overcome personnel and equipment shortages and achieve their objectives. The author's training recommendations are based on the premise that the Active Component forces' primary mission is to fight and win the Nation's wars and their

---

[3] Michele A. Flournoy, "Twelve Strategy Decisions for the Next Administration," *Strategy and Force Planning, Fourth Edition*, ed. Security, Strategy and Forces Faculty, Naval War College (Newport: Naval War College Press, 2004), 34-36.

[4] Todd Harrison, Analysis of the FY 2010 Defense Budget Request, (Washington, DC: Center for Strategic and Budgetary Assessments, 2010), 13.

training should reflect that mission. Further, the author recommends the institutionalization of irregular warfare capabilities within the Reserve Component so that the skills required to prevail in these complex operations are resident within the Total Force. Finally, the author recommends that the formal education of the Total Force must be of the highest priority, especially as the forces are drawn down and there is a smaller talent pool from which to find capability.

The final element where the Armed Forces have historically been found hollow is with the equipment on hand at the time of war. Material hollowing of the Armed Forces has manifested itself, either through worn out and/or obsolete equipment, or simply a lack of equipment on hand. This material hollowing has typically been more acute in the Reserve Component than it has been in the Active Component. The material recommendations proposed to avoid hollowing the near-to-mid term ground forces are based on the need to recapitalize the worn out equipment currently in the inventory and to pursue responsible modernization efforts. These efforts are needed to bring units back up to their Table of Equipment strength to ensure they are properly equipped to accomplish their mission.

It is impossible to categorize any of the following recommendations into a single category because of the interrelationship that policy, personnel, training, and material have with one another. Task Force SMITH, a battalion-sized task force that fought the first American battle of the Korean War, demonstrates the interrelationship of policy, manpower, training, and material within the Armed Forces. The national security policy in 1950 was based on the belief that the next war involving the United States would be a strategic nuclear war with the Soviet Union. As such, that part of the U.S. Army of 1950 assigned to occupation duty in Japan was an acutely drawn-down force prepared to

defend airbases on an island nation where the threat of armor was negligible. Based on

this paradigm, the Army did not equip its occupation forces with sufficient armor nor did

it staff these units sufficiently to train for, much less conduct, major conventional

operations. Consequently, Task Force SMITH was committed to battle as an ad-hoc unit

that did not have the manpower, training or equipment needed to accomplish its assigned

tasks.

The recommendations that follow are an attempt at decreasing national security risks

while, at the same time, increasing the probability of success of achieving the Nation's

objectives. The recommendations are made with the understanding that reduced

resources will mean that there will be diminished capability, and thus increased risk

relative to the force of today. The risk assessment of these recommendations utilizes the

risk assessment framework provided in the 2010 QDR as described below:

> Operational Risk: the ability of the current force to execute strategy successfully within acceptable human, material, financial, and Strategic costs.
> Force Management Risk: the ability to recruit, retain, train, educate, and equip the All-Volunteer Force, and to sustain its readiness and morale
> Institutional Risk: the capacity of management and business practices to plan for, enable, and support the execution of DoD missions.
> Future Challenges Risk: The Department's capacity to execute future missions successfully, and to hedge against shocks.[5]

The author's recommendations seek to provide balance across the different risk

categories by not assuming too much risk in any one category. Each recommendation is

evaluated on the mitigations as well as responsible assumption and management within

---

[5] U.S. DoD, *QDR*, 90.

these risk categories. Key shortfalls are identified and mitigations are detailed. Where no mitigation exists, risk is assumed. In many cases, assuming this risk is the least bad option of many worse options. This is the essence of the non-linear risk management problem.

Recommendation One: Know That Your Future-War Paradigm Is Flawed

It is critical that planners understand that their future-war paradigm is flawed so that they build sufficient flexibility and redundancy into the Armed Forces. Throughout the twentieth-century, the United States has generally been prepared to fight wars. What history shows is that the war the United States was prepared to fight was not the war that it inevitably fought. In 1941, the U.S. Army was postured to fight a war in defense of the Western Hemisphere as evidenced by the assignment of fifty thousand soldiers to the coastal artillery mission within the continental United States. The war it found itself in was major combat in two theaters far away from the United States. In 1950, the U.S. Army in Japan was tasked with the defense of airbases in support of the U.S. Air Force's strategic bombing of the Soviet Union. The war it was fighting by the end of 1950 was a conventional conflict on the Korean peninsula. In 1964, the Army was expected to fight small irregular wars or a conventional war on the plains of Europe; it was not prepared to fight a conventional campaign in the jungles of Vietnam. The Army of 1990 was ready to fight in the defense of Western Europe, but an offensive campaign in the Middle East was completely unexpected. Finally, as late as 2004, the U.S. Armed Forces were still attempting to fight conventional campaigns in Iraq and Afghanistan with insurgencies gaining momentum around them. This most recent case along with the security and stability operations of the 1990's have ushered in the latest of U.S. warfighting paradigms that the conflicts of the future will be irregular wars.

The calls today that conventional warfare is an anachronism are nothing new to U.S. defense planners. This notion has historical precedence throughout the twentieth century and has invariably been proven wrong. A practical, thinking adversary will actively search for ways to negate any advantage the United States may have and adapt their strategy to their advantage. The belief in the 1920's was that the United States had just fought and won "the war to end all wars" and that the world would never again see the carnage that was experienced in the First World War. In fact, the 1928 Kellogg-Briand pact, signed by the United States, United Kingdom, France, Germany, Italy, Japan as well as a number of other nations, actually prohibited the use of war as "an instrument of national policy" except in matters of self-defense.[6] The treaty was essentially invalidated two years later by the 1931 Japanese invasion of Manchuria followed by the Italian invasion of Abyssinia in 1935 and the German invasion of Poland in 1939.

The conventional wisdom in 1950 was that the next war would be a nuclear war with the Soviet Union and U.S force planning after World War II minimized the role that ground forces would play in that war. By the end of that year, however, the U.S. Army was trying to survive the shortcomings of that mistaken paradigm by adapting to fight a conventional war on the Korean peninsula. To the extent a conventional war in the Far

---

[6] United States. "Kellogg-Briand Pact." August 27, 1928. League of Nations Treaty Series, vol. 94, Article 1, (1929).

East had been considered, Vice Admiral C. Turner Joy said simply "we had no plans for this type of war."[7]

The present-day paradigm is evidenced by Department of Defense Directive (DoDD) 3000.07 Irregular Warfare (IW), dated 1 December 2008, that places IW skills on par with those of conventional warfare and establishes as policy that DoD will "maintain capabilities and capacity so that the Department of Defense is as effective in IW as it is in traditional warfare".[8] Department of Defense Instruction (DoDI) 3000.05, Stability Operations, dated 16 September 2009, further reinforces this paradigm by stating, "stability operations are a core U.S. military mission that DoD shall be prepared to conduct with proficiency equivalent to combat operations."[9] While recognizing that many of the capabilities and skills necessary in IW and security operations are applicable to traditional warfare, the shortcoming of DoDD 3000.07 and DoDI 3000.05 is the lack of recognition that many of the capabilities and skills are not applicable and to place these additional tasks on the Armed Forces will equate to a deliberate hollowing of some conventional capabilities and skills. Congressman Ike Skelton (D-MO) recognized this shortcoming when he questioned whether the 2010 Quadrennial Defense Review advocated a force that is "capable of being all things to all contingencies?"[10]

---

[7] Admiral C. Turner Joy, quoted in Paul M. Edwards, *To Acknowledge a War: The Korean War in American Memory.* (Westport, CT: Greenwood Press, 2000), 83.

[8] U.S. Department of Defense, *Department of Defense Directive 3000.07, Irregular Warfare (IW)* (Washington, DC: December 1, 2008), 2.

[9] U.S. Department of Defense, *Department of Defense Instruction 3000.05, Stability Operations* (Washington, DC: September 16, 2009), 2.

[10] Congressman Skelton of Missouri, speaking about the 2010 Quadrennial Defense Review on February 4, 2010, to the House Armed Services Committee, 111th Cong.,2nd sess., H.A.S.C. 111-122, 2.

Despite the current trend lines of threat indicators, force planners must be capable of stepping outside of their present day paradigms and not overcorrect the "past neglect of irregular warfare by rebalancing defense capabilities too far in the direction of fighting the current wars."[11]

Recommendation Two: Publish a National Security Council Document 68 for the 21st Century

The first, and most important, step to drawing down military forces without hollowing out the capabilities of the forces that remain is to design a pragmatic policy that communicates long-term objectives of the United States. Once crafted, this policy can then be used to develop an effective strategy that will then permit force planners to construct a matching military establishment that aligns ends with ways and means.

Since the end of the Cold War, United States security policy has been adrift. The absence of a clearly defined threat combined with the lack of capacity (and/or will) within the international system to deal effectively with emerging crises has had the U.S. oscillating between the roles of global savior and global enforcer.[12] This has translated into an unclear strategy that is interpreted as a requirement for the military to be capable of handling two major regional conflicts simultaneously along with a plethora of security and irregular warfare tasks. Even this requirement, however, has varied to greater and lesser extents over the last twenty years.

---

[11] Patrick M. Cronin, *Restraint: Recalibrating American Strategy* (Washington, DC: Center For A New American Security, June 2008), 8.

[12] Ibid, 7.

Noted strategist Anthony Cordesman believes that the 2010 Quadrennial Defense Review (QDR) and 2010 National Security Strategy (NSS) "provide useful examples of conceptual thinking, but neither provides a real strategy."[13] Instead of clearly defining the desired political ends to develop a strategy that balances the ways and means with those ends, the current documents provide ways and means, but fail to align them with the ends of a policy. This failure to establish a sound policy has created a mismatch between the ends of U.S. security strategy and the means available. For example, current fiscal challenges will limit the United States' ability to "underwrite global security."[14] What is most needed in the twenty-first century is a policy for conducting the Long War that is on par with the policy the U.S. adopted for the conduct of the Cold War.

National Security Council Document (NSC) 68, a Top Secret document written in April 1950, defined the U.S. containment policy of Soviet communism and is probably the closest thing to a grand strategy ever published by the United States. This document led to a number of different strategies for the prosecution of the Cold War, but the original document was just as germane when the Soviet Union collapsed as when it was written. In real world, practical terms it stated U.S. strategic objectives vis-a-vis the Soviet Union, evaluated the security environment, and identified missions the military (as well as the other elements of national power) would need to accomplish to achieve those objectives. In broad terms, NSC 68 realized the ends-means conundrum communist ideology created and presented courses of action to contain this challenge. Recognizing the constrained resources available and the limits of military power, NSC 68 advocated

[13] Anthony H. Cordesman, *US Defense Planning: Creating Reality Based Strategy, Planning, Programming, and Budgeting*, (Washington, DC: Center for Strategic and International Studies, July 2010), 4.

[14] U.S. President. *National Security Strategy*. (Washington, DC: May 2010), 1.

an indirect approach that relied on U.S. values and ideology to defeat the Soviet Union. The collapse of the Soviet Union forty years after publication is testament to the effectiveness that a clearly defined policy can have on achieving national objectives.

Just as in the Cold War, the indirect approach is the only practical way to achieve U.S. national objectives in the Long War. The U.S. military must be able to maintain the capacity to prosecute the Long War over the long term (perhaps decades) to achieve national objectives. Over this time, there will inevitably be successive revolutions in military affairs that will make military forces even more expensive than they currently are. The indirect approach recognizes the limitations of conventional military power in small wars and that there is "no easy solution and that the only sure victory lies in the frustration of the [Islamist] design by the steady development of the moral and material strength of the free world and its projection…in such a way as to bring about an internal change in the [Islamist] system."[15]

There are, however, limitations with the indirect approach. First, a war of ideals will take far longer than the next American election cycle. Second, it counts on the support of allies and assumes that their interests will be aligned with those of the United States. Third, it assumes that other areas of government are effective in and have a comparative advantage over the military element of national power. Finally, the enemy can perceive the indirect approach as weakness and become emboldened.

A comprehensive strategic communications strategy to build support at home and abroad for the Long War is essential to communicating the challenges and objectives of

---

[15] U.S. National Security Council, *National Security Council Document 68* (Washington, DC: April 7, 1950), 53-54. The author substituted [Islamist] for "Communist" in the original NSC 68 to make the point that a policy similar to NSC 68 might be appropriate to the current "Long War."

the Long War and must be an integral part of the indirect strategy. It was forty years and thirteen Presidential administrations after NSC 68 was signed that the Nation fully realized the goals it established. Successive administrations will have to stay on message, but "it is far from clear that the two-and four-year electoral cycles will summon greater bipartisanship and foresight in foreign affairs than we have witnessed during recent campaigns."[16] Winning the hearts and minds of foreign audiences who are unsure of the depth of America's commitment will not be an easy task, but this will prove to be the decisive arena.

The support of allies is critical for the indirect approach to be successful in the Long War. The "U.S. strategy is to employ indirect approaches—primarily through building the capacity of partner governments and their security forces—to prevent the festering problems from turning into crises that require costly and controversial direct military intervention."[17] Building this support will prove to be akin to the burden sharing the costs of containment the United States sought after Vietnam. Garnering the support of Western-style democracies will prove to be the easiest of these endeavors. Gaining the support of peoples in failed and failing states will prove very challenging when their interests are in their immediate needs. Foreign aid, even to unsavory actors on the international scene, should be viewed as a self-defense measure when it supports U.S. interests. The 1971 rapprochement policy that created a tacit strategic anti-Soviet alliance between the People's Republic of China and the United States provides historical

---

[16] Cronin, *Restraint*, 24.

[17] Robert M. Gates, "A Balanced Strategy: Reprogramming the Pentagon for a New Age," *DISAM Journal of International Security Assistance Management* (March 2009; 31, 1; Military Module), 12.

precedence of an indirect approach. Should these efforts fail, the United States must be committed to acting unilaterally when the support of allies falters.

For the indirect approach to be effective, savings that come from cuts to defense spending will have to be reinvested in other elements of national power where the return on investment is assumed higher. With more investment into Department of State and United States Agency for International Development programs, the Department of Defense is able to devote more resources to the primary mission of fighting and winning wars. In a similar vein, there is need for comprehensive interagency reform so that the U.S. military along with the different agencies within the U.S. and coalition governments can achieve a synergy that makes the effects greater than the sum of the individual parts.[18]

To be sure, there will be times and places where the enemy will have to be destroyed. There are intractable elements within the violent extremist movement that can only be dealt with kinetically. These elements will view the indirect approach as weakness in American will to prevail. Again, the strategic communications effort will be paramount in countering enemy propaganda. As Secretary of Defense Gates warned the nation, "it will take the patient accumulation of quiet successes over a long time to discredit and defeat extremist movements and their ideologies."[19]

Richard Rumelt provides ten "common strategy sins" that planners should consider in crafting the modern-day NSC 68; Walter McDougall provides an eleventh in *Can the*

---

[18] The Project on National Security Reform in *Forging a New Shield* provides a detailed analysis of the bold changes required to the national security system to adapt to the changing global security environment. Project on National Security Reform, "Forging a New Shield," (Arlington, VA: Center for the Study of the Presidency, November 2008).

[19] Gates, "A Balanced Strategy," 28.

United States Do Grand Strategy?[20] These considerations, listed in Appendix 1, provide

a framework for constructing the policy for conducting the Long War. Following this

framework ensures that the policy clearly defines attainable strategic goals and focuses

the means available to that end. It is less important *which* policy is adopted than it is to

establish *a* policy that permits strategy to align ends with means and can be clearly

communicated. Whether one wants to contain violent extremist ideology or eradicate it,

is subordinate to having *a* policy in the first place. Following Rumelt's guidance will

ensure that the policy for prosecuting the Long War is pragmatic and, like NSC 68, will

ultimately be successful.

Recommendation Three: Replace the Two Major Regional Conflict (MRC) Paradigm with One MRC Plus Homeland Security, Peacetime Engagement, Forward Presence, and Small Scale Contingency (SSC)

The two major regional conflicts scenario has been the mechanism used to justify the

military force structure the U.S. has maintained for the last twenty years. Instead of

being an interim measure to mitigate strategic surprises after the collapse of the Soviet

Union, this artifact from the Rainbow Five war plan has existed in some form until the

present day.[21] According to Jeffrey Record, the two major regional conflicts scenario

---

[20] The ten "common strategy sins" as presented by Richard Rumelt in CSBA seminar, "Thoughts on Business Strategy," on Sept 25, 2007, cited by Andrew F. Krepinevich and Barry D. Watts in, *Regaining Strategic Competence: Strategy for the Long Haul* (Washington, DC: Center for Strategic and Budgetary Analysis, 2009), x. See Appendix 1 for a list of these "sins".

[21] For a detailed discussion of the Rainbow plans, see Ray S. Cline, *Washington Command Post: The Operations Division* (Washington, DC: Center of Military History, United States Army, 1990), available at http://www.history.army.mil/books/wwii/WCP/ChapterIV.htm, (accessed 24 February 2011) 56-61. For a detailed discussion of the "Germany First" policy and the Plan Dog Memorandum update to Rainbow Five, see Louis G. Morton, *Germany First: The Basic Concept of Allied Strategy in WWII* (Washington, DC: Center of Military History, United States Army, 1990), available at http://www.history.army.mil/books/70-7_01.htm, (accessed 24 February 2011), 35-37.

"speaks more to internal interests of the Armed Forces that it does to the external strategic environment."[22] It was never a prediction the United States would actually face that exigency. The Mid-east and Korea scenarios were merely illustrations of context that emphasized a need for robust strategic mobility rather than specific contingencies.[23] This construct, however, historically improbable, has become economically unsustainable, does not posture the Armed Forces to meet the current strategic challenges and is beyond the realm of "reasonably acceptable strategic risk."[24] The two major regional conflicts force structure pays insufficient attention to counterinsurgency and security and stability operations and incentivizes adversaries to seek asymmetric capabilities to counter U.S. conventional dominance. Although modified by the 2010 QDR to "prevail in a series of overlapping operations of varying character and intensity," and despite the inherent flaws within it, the two major regional conflicts scenario is very much a part of the U.S. military's force structure paradigm.

The justification for the two major regional conflicts scenario suggests that states go to war simply because an opportunity is present and fails to recognize that states go to war only when it is in their interest to do so. History would suggest otherwise; other than World War II, the U.S. has not been engaged in more than one conflict at a time.[25]

---

[22] Jeffrey Record, *The Creeping Irrelevance of U.S. Force Planning* (Carlisle Barracks, PA: Strategic Studies Institute, 1998), 13.

[23] Patrick Clawson, ed., Strategic Assessment 1997 (Washington, DC: National Defense University Institute for Strategic Studies, 1997), 260.

[24] Record, *Creeping Irrelevance*, 14.

[25] The simultaneity of Operations IRAQI and ENDURING FREEDOM (OIF) (OEF) is an obvious exception. It is not included here as an MRC because, according to Amy Belasco in *CRS Report: Troop Levels in the Afghanistan and Iraq Wars, FY2001-FY2012: Cost and Other Potential Issues*, 2 July 2009, 9, U.S. troop levels in OEF were equivalent to a small scale contingency (SSC) operation (10,400) when OIF began.

Maintaining the two-major-regional-conflict force taxes the United States' increasingly finite resources to the point of unsustainability. Replacing the two-major-regional-conflict force with one more suited to the broad range of security challenges on the horizon will mean a reduction in Active Duty endstrength. This implies the United States will have to commit forces judiciously, but is the only way to maintain the capabilities required in the 2010 QDR in a fiscally sustainable way. This approach to force planning recognizes that the U.S. is going to have to learn to do "less with less" and recalibrates U.S. ends and means.[26]

The two-major-regional-conflict force prevents the United States from investing in those areas that are better suited to meeting the current strategic challenges. As directed by the QDR, the military is to "increase capability and capacity for irregular warfare without compromising conventional and nuclear superiority."[27] In the zero-sum game of defense budgets, there will have to be a bill payer for increasing the capacity and capability for irregular warfare. Eliminating the requirement for the second major regional conflict permits those resources to be reinvested in irregular warfare capabilities or saved.

It can be argued that the current situations in Iran and North Korea demand a two-major-regional-conflict-force structure, but in the event the U.S. was committed militarily in Iran, the defense of South Korea would be an entirely different proposition than it was in 1950. First, the South Korean military is a very capable, professional military force; the economic conditions in the two Koreas now have been reversed since 1950; and the

---

[26] Cronin, *Restraint*, 11.

[27] U.S. DoD, *QDR*, 103.

North Koreans cannot sustain an offensive into South Korea without support from the Chinese or Russians. International condemnation would make any outside support highly unlikely in the case of North Korean aggression. Finally, nuclear retaliation in the event of North Korean invasion of South Korea provides a viable option that should be considered.

The argument that the two-major-regional-conflict force provides enough forces to handle a near-peer competitor is also illogical. China is unlikely to develop the conventional capabilities in the near-to-mid term to challenge the United States in a conventional conflict. China is leading the way with thinking about asymmetric uses of its capabilities and rather than trying to compete head on, they appear determined to alter the rules.[28] The United States' thinking about war with China should focus on regional access during a crisis. Gaining this access will require more reliance on the diplomatic and economic elements of national power rather than greater military means.[29] Furthermore, the U.S. aversion to a ground war on the mainland of Asia should translate into investments of naval, air and amphibious forces; those forces that provide access and freedom of action in the Japanese and South China Seas and are the same forces that provided the foundation of Imperial Japan's defeat in 1945.[30]

Replacing the two major regional conflict force structure with one built around a single major regional conflict plus homeland security, peacetime engagement, forward presence, and small scale contingency would knowingly assume additional risk, but

---

[28] Cronin, *Restraint*, 22.

[29] Ibid.

[30] Record, *Creeping Irrelevance*, 17.

available air and sea striking power for aggression in another theater make that risk "prudent and manageable."[31]

Risk Assessment

Replacing the two major regional conflicts force structure model, as described, assumes some degree of future challenges risk in that U.S. force structure could be inadequate to meet the challenges of two simultaneous major regional conflicts. This risk is mitigated by the "declining incidence of large-scale interstate warfare" and the dominance the U.S. maintains in its long-range strike and nuclear-deterrent capabilities.[32]

Recommendation Four: Remodel the Total Force with an Emphasis on the Reserve Component Roles and Missions

Remodeling the Total Force toward a structure that places a premium on the role of the Reserve Component is not a new concept. In fact, it has been seriously looked at after every period of extended conflict in the twentieth century and is very similar to the military establishment President Truman envisioned in 1949.[33] Although not well trained or equipped, the National Guard was the largest component of the U.S. Army between 1922 and 1939. Reservists accounted for sixty eight percent of the U.S. Marine Corps Total Force by the end of World War II.[34] The Total Force Concept of August 1970, which was declared policy by Secretary of Defense Schlesinger in 1973, increased the

---

[31] Gates, "A Balanced Strategy," 13.

[32] Record, *Creeping Irrelevance*, 13.

[33] Robert J. Donovan, *Conflict and Crisis, The Presidency of Harry S Truman, 1945-1948* (New York: WW Norton and Company, 1977), 137.

[34] William Navas, "Integration of the Active and Reserve Navy: A Case for Transformational Change," Naval Reserve Association, 51 (May 2004): 5; Reserve Officers of Public Affairs Unit 4-1, The Marine Corps Reserve: A History, 59.

reliance on the Reserve Component due to reductions in the active component (AC) force structure. The main distinction with the author's proposal compared with those of past periods is that the concept of the operational reserve, where Reserve forces participate routinely and regularly in ongoing military missions, be institutionalized into U.S. military culture.

Throughout the twentieth century the role of the reserves has been that of a strategic reserve – that is to provide strategic depth to the Active Component forces in the event of a major war. Reserve forces have not been committed in this capacity since the Korean War and their contribution to the Nation's war efforts since that time has been little value added. Throughout the twentieth century, the ability of the Reserves to attain combat readiness "remained open to serious question."[35] When the strategic reserve has been mobilized, it was invariably found lacking the readiness required to fight. In the 1950's, there was no requirement for reservists to serve in the Army and most units were not sufficiently trained for rapid mobilization in an emergency.[36] Assignments to units were frequently made without regard to military specialty. In 1961, the United States mobilized 120,000 reservists to beef up the North Atlantic Treaty Organization and found them lacking in readiness.[37] Reserve utilization in the Vietnam War and Operation

---

[35] U.S. Army Center of Military History, "American Military History, Volume 2, Chapter 9, The Army of the Cold War From the New Look to Flexible Response," 263.

[36] Ibid., 262.

[37] U.S. Army Center of Military History, "American Military History, Volume 2, Chapter 10, The U.S. Army in Vietnam Background, Buildup, and Operations, 1950-1967," 294.

DESERT STORM was minimal and their contribution to those war efforts was, at best, limited.[38]

The contribution of the Reserve Component to the Nation's war efforts changed after the attacks on September 11, 2001. Since that time, the Reserve Component has served in an operational capacity, deploying alongside their active duty counterparts in Operations ENDURING and IRAQI FREEDOM as well as other contingency operations at home and abroad. In this capacity, the Reserve Component has performed remarkably and has provided the required depth for U.S. ground combat forces to sustain operations for over nine years. This reliance on the operational reserve to meet national security requirements "should continue and should grow even after the demands for forces associated with current operations are reduced."[39]

The institution of the All-Volunteer Force in the 1970's was the first step toward an operational reserve. "In rejecting the Vietnam-era paradigm [using draftees to meet manpower requirements before calling up the reserves], Congress and the Nixon Administration ensured that in future conflicts reservists would be the first force called up when there was a need to supplement active duty volunteers..."[40] The notion of utilization of the Reserve Component in an operational capacity developed almost by default, in response to current and projected needs for operations in Iraq and Afghanistan and the associated force generation requirements.[41] The U.S. military is currently at a

---

[38] Commission on the National Guard and Reserves, Transforming the National Guard and Reserves Into a 21st Century Operational Force, Final Report to Congress and Secretary of Defense (Arlington, VA: January 31, 2008), E-7, E-8.

[39] Ibid., 5.

[40] Ibid., E-8.

[41] Ibid., 6.

crossroads with regard to the operational reserve. Despite the significant contributions the operational reserve has made to the Global War on Terror and the rhetoric about the fundamental changes to the military required to make this a viable component of the Total Force, the institutional reforms required have not been implemented. The indecisiveness of DoD's commitment to the operational reserve is evident in the language of the QDR: "Preventing and deterring conflict will likely necessitate the continued use of some elements of the reserve component…in an operational capacity well into the future."[42] Additionally, funding for operational reserve requirements is provided through supplemental appropriations and not a part of the regular Program Objective Memorandum cycle. Whether this concept is institutionalized or not remains to be seen, but the Commission on the National Guard and Reserve concludes, "there is no reasonable alternative to the nation's continued increased reliance on reserve components as part of its operational force for missions at home and abroad."[43] Roles and missions will need to be further defined by the upcoming DoD roles and mission review in spring 2011 so that the current model can be sustained over the longer term.

The lower overall personnel and operating costs of the Reserve Component make for a larger Total Force for a given budget.[44] Reserve Component forces are less expensive than their Active Component counterparts: a Reserve Component member costs approximately fifteen percent of an Active Component member when not mobilized.[45] A

---

[42] U.S. DoD, *QDR*, 53.

[43] CNGR, "Transforming the National Guard and Reserves," 5.

[44] U.S. DoD, *QDR*, 53.

[45] Government Accountability Office, *GAO-07-828, Military Personnel: DOD Needs to Establish a Strategy and Improve Transparency Over Reserve and National Guard Compensation to Manage Significant Growth in Cost, June 2007* (Washington, DC: Government Printing Office), 21 and 41.

non-operationally employed Army National Guard Brigade Combat Team (BCT) costs twenty-eight percent of that of an active duty BCT. The cost of that same brigade goes up to 136 percent of the active duty BCT during the year of mobilization (including eight months of operational employment). Taken over a five-year force generation cycle, the National Guard BCT costs are just under fifty percent of the active duty BCT over the same five-year period.[46]

Reserve Component forces provide unique capabilities to the Long War that cannot be matched by their Active Component counterparts without sacrificing capabilities in the Active Component primary mission of fighting and winning the Nation's wars. The civilian skill sets that Reserve Component members contribute to counterinsurgency and security and stability operations are not easily acquired and maintained by the Active Component. The Reserve Component provides a link to the communities in which they live, which makes them uniquely suited for homeland security and consequence management responsibilities. Even while serving in an operational capacity, the Reserve Component still provides strategic depth for the Nation in the event Active Component forces are insufficient to handle emerging crises. Despite the advantages an operational Reserve Component brings to the national security arena, challenges to sustainment remain in the form of manning and legacy policies.

Reserve Component forces are uniquely suited to be the first force of choice for counterinsurgency and security and stability operations. The skill sets Reserve Component forces can provide a Combatant Commander make them uniquely qualified

---

[46] CNGR, "Transforming the National Guard and Reserves," 66. Although the CNGR does not believe the cost data used for their study offers "conclusive evidence on the overall relative costs of the reserve and active components, it does offer insight into how DoD could explore rebalancing to meet the demands of the new security environment."

to conduct these operations. Professional police officers provide training, experience and perspective on patrolling in a counterinsurgency environment that an infantryman might not acquire. Prison guards, lawyers, judges and small business owners are able to communicate nuances about the rule of law and economic development that Active Component forces cannot acquire with any amount of training. The performance of Reserve Component forces in current operations indicates they are more than capable of assuming persistent forward engagement missions. The proposed Humanitarian Assistance Special Purpose Marine Air Ground Task Force, the Unit Deployment Program and other forward deployed missions can be carried out by the Reserve Component forces equally as well as Active Component forces.[47] Besides capitalizing on these skill sets, assigning Reserve Component forces to these missions permits the Active Component forces to better train and prepare for the next conventional war.

Reserve Component forces provide a flexibility to respond rapidly in the United States that can be efficiently increased in times of need, and then reduced in a way that economically preserves that capability when requirements diminish.[48] In other words, Reserve forces provide capability that is paid for only when needed. Reserve Component forces are forward-deployed in the homeland and their skills combined with military training and organization provide advantages that local governments and the Active Component cannot provide These ties with the American public, at least theoretically, ensures public support for potentially extended Long War efforts.

---

[47] The HASPMAGTF is a proposal to deploy a battalion-sized task force in the EUCOM AOR (presumably Rota, Spain) to be in position to respond to humanitarian assistance and disaster relief missions as well as partner capacity-building missions. These forces would rotate every six months.

[48] CNGR, "Transforming the National Guard and Reserves,", 5.

Using the reserve in an operational capacity does nothing to take away from the strategic depth reserve forces provide to national security and actually enhances the Reserve Component's readiness in the event a strategic mobilization is required. As noted earlier, the major shortcoming of the strategic reserve throughout the twentieth century was with inadequate readiness levels when mobilized. Regular training cycles will maintain critical military skills and improve the Reserve Component's ability to meet a variety of mission tasks. The experience Reserve Component forces gain while serving in an operational capacity is difficult to quantify, but will prove invaluable in the event a strategic mobilization is required. Having one-fifth of the Reserve Component mobilized at any one time will only enhance the readiness of the Reserve Component as a whole and avoid repeating the inadequacies of past mobilizations. Exchange agreements between states will be necessary to cover any gaps created by the operational deployments of National Guard forces.

An examination of the benefits that the Reserve Component has provided to the Nation reveals that a strategic Reserve Component does not provide the same return on investment as an operational reserve. Until the World Trade Center attack in 2001, the Reserve Component had not mobilized in large numbers since the Korean War. Comparing the number of duty days (in millions) of contributions the Reserve Component has made to national defense reveals that the strategic reserve did not provide the same return on investment that an operational reserve has provided. Total Guard and Reserve spending in 1986 was 5.8 percent of the total defense budget ($30.1 billion for reserves out of the $511.9 billion total in 2008 dollars), with the RC providing 0.9 million duty days of service. In contrast, Reserve Component contributions in an operational capacity during 2005 were 68.3 million duty days for approximately 6.1 percent of the total defense budget ($33.6 billion for reserves out of the $548.8 total in 2008 dollars).[49]

Philosophical reasons provide further justification of emphasizing the role of the Reserve Component as the first force of choice for counterinsurgency and security and stability operations. The use of citizen soldiers as the vanguard of the indirect approach strengthens the bridge between the American people and their military and further integrates the Armed Forces with the society they serve. It makes the Long War more than simply a military issue when Small-Town, U.S.A. sends its sons and daughters off to foreign lands to fight the Nation's battles and harnesses the unquantifiable moral elements that Carl Von Clausewitz described as "the precious metal, the real weapon."[50] There is power in the message that communicates to both domestic and international actors that the United States is committed to winning the Long War through the furthering of U.S. values. In the context of the elements of strategy – ends, ways and means - the means (citizen soldiers) contribute to different ways simultaneously (direct threat as well as indirect pressure). By committing to the expansion and institutionalization of an operational Reserve Component, "the world will see that the strength of this nation is found in the character and dedication and courage of everyday citizens."[51]

---

[49] Office of the Secretary of Defense (Comptroller), *National Defense Budget Estimates for 2008* (Washington, DC: March 2007), 71, 73, and 81 and John Nagl and Travis Sharp, *An Indispensible Force: Investing in America's National Guard and Reserves* (Washington, DC: Center for New American Security, September 2010), 22.

[50] Carl Von Clausewitz, On War, ed. and trans. Michael Howard and Peter Paret (New York, NY 1993), 217.

[51] U.S. President, "Guard and Reserves 'Define Spirit of America,'" (Remarks by the President of the United States to Employees at the Pentagon, September 17, 2001, available at www.whitehouse.gov/news/releases/2001/09/ 20010917-3.html).

The fact that the Reserve Component is currently being used as an operational force does not make it a sustainable option. The reserve components were not established to be employed on a rotational basis. Key underlying laws, regulations, policies, funding mechanisms, pay categories, mobilization processes, and personnel rules that manage the reserve components will have to be modified to support their evolution into such an operational force.[52] To continue using the reserves in an operational capacity, the funding of mobilizations will need to be moved from supplemental funding and included in the base budget. Not doing so leaves the concept of the operational reserve a year-to-year decision and prohibits this capacity from maturing into viable operational force.[53] Implementing those improvements outlined in the Commission of the National Guard and Reserve's 2008 report, *Transforming the National Guard and Reserves Into a 21st Century Operational Force, Final Report to Congress and Secretary of Defense,* will ensure that the Nation can sustain an operational reserve over the long term.

A larger Reserve Component is required to sustain the rotational employment required of an operational force. To sustain the Reserve Component in an operational capacity, reserve forces need to be staffed at a level that supports a one to five deployment-to-dwell time ratio as directed by Department of Defense Instruction 1235.12, *Accessing the Reserve Components.*[54] This provides reservists and their civilian employers the requisite predictability and affords the time needed to get through the force generation model. Staffing levels for the Reserve Component need to be expanded to guarantee

---

[52] CNGR, "Transforming the National Guard and Reserves," 10.

[53] Government Accountability Office, GAO-09-989, Reserve Forces Army Needs to Finalize on Implementation Plan and Funding Strategy for Sustaining an Operational Reserve, (Washington, DC: Government Printing Office, September 2009), 35.

[54] U.S. Department of Defense, Department of Defense Instruction 1235.12, Accessing the Reserve Components (Washington, DC: February 4, 2010), 2.

continuous access to this force in operational capacity. Access to these forces will provide the critical lever for meeting global operational demands while allowing active duty endstrength to be drawn down.[55] Although beyond the scope of this paper, staffing levels could hypothetically be based on homeland security and Combatant Command Phase Zero engagement requirements with additional force structure to account for counterinsurgency operations and security and stability operations.

It has become too expensive for the United States to maintain a military force capable of doing everything that is being asked of it. Combat units are focusing their efforts on stability and counterinsurgency tasks that are affecting their ability to maintain proficiency in their core competencies. To ensure that units are trained in all tasks, personnel increases were needed in 2007 to provide the operations tempo relief that would permit forces to get through training cycles. Rather than trying to create a force that is "all things to all contingencies," the Department of Defense should task the different components with separate core competencies. This permits each component to maximize the unique skills they provide to national security. Those core competencies can then be institutionalized within the Total Force so that the integration of those forces can achieve synergistic effects.[56]

Remodeling the Total Force as described permits drawing down Active Component forces to meet the most likely immediate and long-term conventional threats. An expanded Reserve Component then provides the sustaining power of the armed forces and mitigates the loss in capability. Active duty force structure should be built around

---

[55] U.S. Department of Defense, *Quadrennial Defense Review Report*. (Washington, DC: February 2010), 102.

[56] Congressman Skelton of Missouri, speaking about the 2010 Quadrennial Defense Review on February 4, 2010, to the House Armed Services Committee, 111th Cong.,2nd sess., H.A.S.C. 111-122, 2.

the most dangerous Combatant Command Operations Plan plus a share of the forward presence and small-scale contingency requirements. This reduction in active duty endstrength will be the bill payer for the expanded Reserve Component.

To meet the one major regional conflict requirement, Active Component force structure needs to be based off the most robust Operations Plan requirement of the Combatant Commanders with additional forces to meet diplomatic commitments and small-scale contingency requirements. Force structure should be sufficient to achieve a desired deployment-to-dwell ratio of one to three so the Active Component can meet training, education and reconstitution obligations. There should also be sufficient force built in (approximately eighteen percent) to fill trainee, transient, holdee and student billets without sacrificing the capabilities in combat units.

Although further research is required to determine the optimal balance between the Active and Reserve Component forces, a notional example of the rebalanced force would essentially reverse the force structure currently in place. Instead of forty-five Active Component brigade combat teams (BCTs) and twenty-eight Reserve Component BCTs; the new mix would be twenty-eight Active Component BCTs and forty-five Reserve Component BCTs. The Marine Corps could convert one Active Component division into Reserve Component structure. Rebalancing to this degree would produce operating force savings of approximately fifteen percent over the five-year force generation cycle.[57] This structure would be the starting point and once actual force requirements are determined,

---

[57] According to CNGR, an Active Component (AC) BCT costs approximately $1 billion dollars per year or $5 billion over five years. Based on CNGR data, a Reserve Component (RC) BCT would cost $2.48 billion dollars over the same five-year period (one force generation cycle). A Total Force mix of 45 AC and 28 RC BCTs costs $2.944 trillion dollars over years whereas a Total Force mix of 28 AC and 45 RC BCTs costs $2.516 trillion. This yields a savings of $4.284 trillion, or 14.5% over the five-year period.

additional Active Component units could be converted to the Reserve Component. Additional conversion of units would be a one-for-one swap i.e. when an Active Component unit deactivates; another like-size unit is commissioned within the Reserve Component. Converting Active Component forces to the Reserve Component in this manner preserves structure within the Total Force while reducing costs.

Such a significant drawdown of Active Component forces must be an iterative process. Drawing down forces too quickly risks creating a gap in capability that results in vulnerability. Leadership must avoid an obsession with disarmament once the process begins. During the drawdown of the 1920's, once the rush to disarm the military was on, it was nearly impossible to stop. The mindset was so pervasive that, despite the numerous indicators and warnings of impending danger, a bill to prevent demobilizing more than two-thirds of the Army squeezed through the House of Representatives by a margin of a single vote in August 1941.[58] Members departing the Active Component must be properly incentivized to join the Reserve Component so that the Total Force can capitalize on the experience the personnel have gained over the last nine years.

A reduced Active Component will be a forcing function for leadership to come up with creative solutions for the indirect approach to the Long War. Smaller Active Component forces would limit the means available to be used at any one time and would force a prioritization of issues that warrant the commitment of U.S. ground forces. In the near-to-mid term, the U.S. military can drawdown its Active Component forces from a position of relative conventional military strength.

---

[58] C. Joseph Bernado and Eugene H. Bacon, Ph. D., American Military Policy: Its Development Since 1775 (Harrisburg: The Telegraph Press, 1961), 423.

Risk Assessment

The smaller Active Component force available for deployment at any given time does increase the force structure and future challenges risks associated with this recommendation. Despite having one-fifth of the Reserve Component mobilized and ready for tasking at all times, remodeling the Total Force, as described in the notional example, would decrease the total number of BCTs available for tasking by twenty-six percent.[59] The reduced personnel costs, however, mitigate the force structure risk and institutional risk by freeing funds and investing in modernization and force preservation initiatives.

Recommendation Five: Rebalance the Roles and Missions within the Active and Reserve Components

This recommendation is broken down into two subsets: that the Active Component primarily exists to fight and win the Nation's wars and that counterinsurgency and security and stability operations should be institutionalized within the Reserve Component. Further, the development of a force generation model that trains the Reserve Component to their mission essential tasks within the limited time available is critical to ensuring success. It attempts to capitalize on the unique capabilities that the Active and Reserve Components contribute to national security and considers that force design is as

---

[59] A Total Force mix of 45 Active Component (AC) and 28 Reserve Component (RC) BCTs (1/5 of which are mobilized at any one time) equates to 50 BCTs available for tasking. The author's recommendation of 28 AC BCTs and 45 RC BCTs equates to only 37 BCTs available for tasking at any one time. The delta of 13 BCTs equals 26%.

important as force size. It is based on the premises that the Active Component exists, "first and foremost, to fight conventional wars" and that the cultural and training differences between the Active and Reserve Components make the Reserve Component better qualified to conduct counterinsurgency and security and stability operations.[60]

Active Component Forces Primarily Exist to Fight and Win the Nation's Conventional Wars

Training for counterinsurgency and security and stability operations has historically robbed active duty soldiers of their ability to conduct conventional campaigns. The 1933 Civilian Conservation Corps (CCC) provides a notable historical example of this deliberate hollowing of conventional military capability. Assignment to the CCC did provide some officers and non-commissioned officers with administration experience, but tactical units were stripped of their leadership and "unit training came to a halt and the Army's readiness for immediate employment was nearly destroyed."[61] The American occupation force in Japan in 1950 did very little training in conventional tasks and was completely unprepared for war in Korea. Land army tasks of static warfare in mid-1953 degraded Marine Corps amphibious readiness to between twenty-five and sixty percent.[62] In 1999, the Army reported that twenty percent of the Active Component divisions (two

---

[60] Ian F.W. Becket, ed., The Roots of Counterinsurgency: Armies and Guerilla Warfare 1900-1945 (London: Blandford Press, 1988), 15.

[61] U.S. Army Center of Military History, "American Military History, Volume 2, Chapter 2, Between World Wars," 63.

[62] J. Robert Moskin, *The U.S. Marine Corps Story, Third Revised Edition* (Boston: Little, Brown and Company, 1992), 587.

of ten) were no longer combat ready to fight major conventional war because of a personnel draw down and deployments to peace operations.[63]

The Nation maintains a standing Army to be prepared to fight its conventional wars even when the Nation does not expect it to do so. This requirement is no less important today than it has been throughout the twentieth-century. According to Secretary of Defense Robert Gates: "the images of Russian tanks rolling into Georgia last August [2008] were a reminder that nation-states and their militaries do still matter."[64] In this sense, Active Component forces should be viewed as a national insurance policy. Assigning Active Component forces missions that do not contribute to their ability to wage conventional campaigns erodes their capability to do so and, over the long term, threatens their warrior culture. Because these forces cannot achieve the level of mastery in skills required for success in the Long War without sacrificing conventional capabilities, Active Component training must focus on large-scale, combined-arms, forcible-entry operations. The Active Component's specialty is expeditionary combat operations on short notice and the lethality of the modern battlefield is very unforgiving of units who are not well trained in this form of warfare.

Time is perhaps the most precious resource available to a military. No amount of resourcing can overcome the limitations time places on military preparations for the next war. "It takes time and effort to master the skill set that each [conventional and irregular war] requires and each approach demands exclusive share of some overlapping

---

[63] Hans Binnendijk and Stuart E. Johnson, eds., *Transforming for Stabilization and Reconstruction Operations* (Washington, DC: National Defense University Press, 2004), 88.

[64] Gates, "A Balanced Strategy," 28.

resources."[65] Active Component training for counterinsurgency, and security and stability operations takes time away from its core competencies, that when gone, can never be regained. Additionally, as Active Component forces are drawn down, their training in any competency will be at a premium. Therefore, it is imperative that as Active Component forces are drawn down, they are afforded the opportunity to train to their primary mission.

Combined arms and maneuver warfare place a premium on speed and overwhelming firepower at the decisive point to shatter the enemy's cohesion and compel him to do your will. Training for these types of operations reinforce the goal of placing ordnance on target at the right time; the faster it can be done, the better. These characteristics, however, are diametrically opposed to the characteristics of the training required to be successful in counterinsurgency and security and stability operations where firepower is the instrument of last, rather than first, resort. The tasks of building wells and restoring electrical power to a community require doctrinal and training reprogramming of Active Component forces to be done effectively. As evidenced today, institutionalizing this capability within the Active Component without hollowing its conventional capabilities is not feasible without further resourcing (i.e. manpower).

This recommendation is not proposing there should not be cross training among core competencies. The Active Component must be prepared to conduct counterinsurgency and security and stability operations because they will most likely be the first responders to an emerging crisis. Additionally, these operations provide valuable experience to forces that cannot be replicated in training. According to Richard Lacquement, "Any

---

[65] Richard H. Lacquement Jr, "In the Army Now" The American Interest Online, September-October 2010, http://www.the-american-interest.com/article.cfm?piece=860 (accessed 10 October 2010)

hedging strategy that balances the need for conventional and irregular warfare capabilities needs to include some reasonable means to scale capabilities up or down."[66] The current construct of just-in-time training for counterinsurgency and security and stability operations skills has proven sufficient over the last nine years and provides a reasonable model to use in the future. The operational Reserve Component would then be used to provide depth for longer-term stability operations and permit the Active Component to resume its role as a force in readiness.

Institutionalize Counterinsurgency and Security and Stability Operations into the Expanded Operational Reserve Component

Institutionalizing counterinsurgency and security and stability operations competencies in the Reserve Component provides the balance required for the Total Force to be successful in prosecuting the Long War. The U.S. has dedicated Special Forces, cyber warfare forces and strategic deterrent forces. It would seem that dedicated counterinsurgency and security and stability operations forces are the next logical step in the evolution of twenty-first century force structure planning. Under this construct, the Reserve Component would become United States' first force of choice for counterinsurgency and security and stability operations. Since force design is equally important to force size, the majority of forces in the expanded Reserve Component should be recruited into those skill sets needed to prosecute counterinsurgency and security and stability operations. Security and stability operations require little in the way of combined-arms maneuver, so military police, civil affairs, chemical/biological warfare

---

[66] Lacquement, "In the Army Now."

units, engineers, and border security should make up a large portion of the Reserve Component.[67]

To train the Reserve Component to handle adequately the myriad tasks and additional responsibilities, they must have a force generation model that ensures they receive the required training. To be effective, this model should maximize the operational employment of forces during the mobilization period by focusing on developing core competencies during premobilization training. It must have enough flexibility built in to adjust to the current strategic environment and allow forces to train to a specific mobilization requirement. Just as the Active Component requires some competency in counterinsurgency and security and stability operations, the Reserve Component needs to have the ability to conduct combined arms training. The force generation model must provide enough exposure to these operations for the Reserve Component to remain a viable force in the event of a strategic mobilization.

The force generation model for the operational reserve needs to take into account the diversity of tasks required and mission essential tasks should be tailored to provide sufficient exposure to different skill sets. A notional force generation model is provided in Figure 1. In this notional model, Year One tasks include resetting the forces to recover from mobilization and work on consequence management tasks. The focus for Year Two is on conventional warfare and combined-arms skills in which the RC must maintain competency. Years Three and Four are mirror images of each other and they focus on irregular warfare skill sets. The mobilization period is Year Five, which includes a six-month training work up followed by a six-month deployment. This model is presented

---

[67] Record, *Creeping Irrelevance*, 11.

only as an illustration; different forces would task organize their force generation model based on their mission essential tasks. Additionally, forward engagement missions could be covered by United States based alert forces or training mobilizations. The advantage of constructing a force generation model in this fashion is that the Nation always has at least one-fifth of its Reserve Component trained in each of the competencies in the event of a strategic or emergency mobilization.

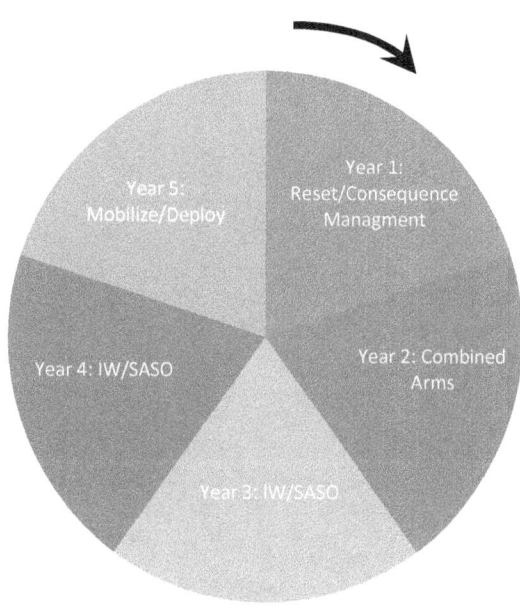

Figure 1: Notional Reserve Component Force Generation Model

Risk Assessment

Rebalancing the roles and missions of the Active and Reserve Components, as described, mitigates future challenges and operations risks by providing specially trained forces for the contingencies they face. It permits defense planners to "mold ground

49

forces into a shape that best suits official policy without having to prepare for every threat."[68] Some operations risk is assumed, as forces will inevitably be tasked with missions outside of their core competencies. This risk can be mitigated by training and educating the force to be able to adapt quickly to the situation. This is discussed in more detail in Recommendation Seven.

This recommendation will require the Active and Reserve Components to redefine how they view one another. The cultural and structural differences between the Active and Reserve Components create a degree of animosity between them, especially when it comes to competing for resources. In many cases, these differences are based in law and are more than just perceptions that need to be changed. Although significant progress has been made in recent years, civilian and military leadership alike will need to remain firmly committed to integrating both components into the Total Force to ensure success.

Recommendation Six: Pursue Responsible Modernization Efforts

Throughout the twentieth-century, defense planners have repeatedly looked to military modernization programs for savings when the Department of Defense has experienced budget cuts. A review of this history reveals that a failure to keep military modernization on a steady progression only defers and increases the cost of modernization in the long run. This is evidenced today by the criticality of the state of all classes of ground forces' equipment brought on by the historically low levels of funding dedicated to modernization during the procurement holiday of the 1990's and exacerbated by the

---

[68] U.S. Army Center of Military History, "American Military History, Volume 2, Chapter 9, The Army of the Cold War From the New Look to Flexible Response" 251.

accelerated equipment wear-out rates caused by the wars in Iraq and Afghanistan. This has created a military of today that is essentially a service-life extended military of the 1980's.[69] Therefore, it is imperative that current defense planners look beyond the short-term savings of cutting modernization programs and pursue responsible modernization efforts that maintain a long-term view.

At the beginning of World War II, equipment needs for the U.S. Army had to come from World War I vintage stockpiles due to the limited interwar investments in replacing worn out equipment. The "manpower first" policies of the U.S. Army of the 1920's and 1930's allocated only 5.6% of the defense budget for modernization and replacement of arms and equipment for the ground elements of the Army and forced a reliance on World War I surpluses to meet training and readiness requirements.[70] These policies continued to the eve of World War II where research and development accounted for only 0.8% of War Department budget in 1939 because these funds were frozen to pay for the Initial Protective Force.[71] This occurred at a time when technology was changing at such a rapid pace that many of the weapons systems the Army went to war with in World War II were obsolete.[72]

Since procurement budgets are projected to fall in real terms over the next ten years, defense planners are again going to be challenged with modernizing the Armed Forces in

---

[69] Mackenzie Eaglen, "Backgrounder, No 2418, 7 June 2010, U.S. Defense Spending: The Mismatch Between Plans and Resources," The Heritage Foundation, http://report.heritage.org/bg2418 (accessed 1 July 2010)

[70] David E. Johnson, "From Frontier Constabulary to Modern Army: The U.S. Army Between the World Wars," in *The Challenge of Change, Military Institutions and New Realities, 1918-1941*, ed. Harold R. Winton and David R. Mets (Lincoln, NE: University of Nebraska Press, 2000), 182.

[71] Ibid., 183.

[72] U.S. Army Center of Military History, "American Military History, Volume 2, Chapter 2, Between World Wars," 69.

an era of fiscal scarcity.[73] In order to avoid repeating the past modernization mistakes,

defense planners should focus on those programs that allow the military to shoot, move

and communicate more effectively. The current conventional dominance of United States

ground forces and the absence of a peer competitor provide planners with an opportunity

to modernize the force in a fiscally responsible manner. Procurement does not have to be

in the most expensive weapons systems, but the chosen programs must permit combat on

reasonably favorable terms under any circumstances.[74] Jeffrey Record makes this point

in *The Creeping Irrelevance of U.S. Force Planning:*

> Maintenance of conventional supremacy does not dictate the buying of
> large quantities of each and every high-tech weapons system that comes
> along; strategic urgency vanished with the Soviet Union, and the United
> States can be more selective in the choice and timing of large military
> hardware production commitments. But it does require maintenance of
> significant conventional forces as well as robust and unstinting investment
> in research, development, testing, and integration of . . . technologies.[75]

Modernization efforts should also be made without regard to whether the programs are

intended for the conventional Active Component forces or the Reserve Component

forces. Allowing either the Active or Reserve Component to get too far ahead of the

other in terms of modernization will prove to be counterproductive. Following the

previous recommendations will require that the Active and Reserve Components are

complementary in their capabilities. The differences in the core competencies of the

components will dictate that the components cannot be completely interoperable, but

those elements that share competencies must be standardized to the maximum extent

---

[73] Congressional Budget Office, *Long Term Implications of FY10 Defense Budget,* (Washington, DC: Congressional Budget Office, January 2010), 2.

[74] U.S. War Office, *Report of the Secretary of War to the President, 1933* (Washington, DC: Government Printing Office, 1933), 31.

[75] Record, *Creeping Irrelevance,* 19.

possible. This will insure that next-to-deploy units have the most modern equipment for training and meeting operational requirements.

Risk Assessment

Pursuing modernization efforts, even during periods of tightening defense budgets is essential to mitigating future challenges risk. Failure to do so places U.S. ground forces in the same position they were in at the beginning of World War II. Additionally, deferring modernization while waiting for technological advancements to mature may mean assuming risk in current operations.

Recommendation Seven: Invest in the Education of Total Force

The Professional Military Education of the Total Force is the foundation upon which the military as an institution build the intellectual capacity to adapt to and confront reality. Peter Gizewski states in *Army 2040 The Global Security Environment: Emerging Trends and Potential Challenges* that "perhaps the most crucial component for ensuring an effective response to the challenges of tomorrow resides in the intellectual or conceptual realm."[76] As such, to avoid hollowing a much smaller Active Component military, investments in professional military education (PME) must remain of the highest priority during a drawdown period. Current and future PME should include increased focus on counterinsurgency and security and stability operations in the

---

[76] Peter J. Gizewski, "Army 2040 The Global Security Environment: Emerging Trends and Potential Challenges" (Paper prepared for the Annual Meeting of the Canadian Political Science Association, Carleton University, Ottawa, Canada, 27 May 2009), 15.

curricula, provide expanded opportunities for both the Active and Reserve components, and promote vigorous experimentation with new concepts and technologies.

History provides examples where, during times of fiscal restraint, the U.S. military has allowed the military's education system to fall into disrepair. In 1927, Maj. Gen. Johnson Hagood stated, "our unpreparedness did not come from a lack of money, lack of soldiers or lack of supplies. It came from a lack of brains, or perhaps it would be fair to say, lack of genius."[77] Additionally, between 1938 and 1939 the curriculum of the U.S. Army's Command and General Staff School had 198 hours of instruction on the vintage infantry division of World War I; 29 hours of instruction for mechanized warfare; 13 hours of aviation instruction; and 13 hours dedicated to equitation.[78] Just two years later, the combined-arms, mechanized warfare of World War II proved how out of balance the Command and General Staff School's curriculum was with the changing characteristics of warfare.

To ensure that the Armed Forces do not suffer from a "lack of genius" in future wars, the U.S. military needs to be responsible for doing its own thinking. The officer corps must be able to provide the intellectual dynamism required to come up with creative solutions for the complex and diverse threats of the twenty-first century. To encourage thinking outside of traditional military realms, opportunities for graduate education at major universities would provide officers with a broader educational experience than they can get from service schools. Incentivizing teaching posts at the service schools and war colleges would ensure that best and brightest are provided an opportunity to take an

---

[77] Winton and Mets, *The Challenge of Change*, 163.

[78] Brigadier General L.J. McNair to the Adjutant General, 31 August 1939, Subject: Annual Report, School Year 1938-1939, in U.S. Army Command and General Staff Library collection as quoted in Winton and Mets, *The Challenge of Change*, 185-186.

intellectual journey into warfare that is impossible outside of academic institutions. Further, the military needs to write its own doctrine; the loss of the intellectual rigor by subcontracting this critical requirement goes far beyond the manpower savings the military gets in return.

The wars in Iraq and Afghanistan have forced the military to recognize the significance of human terrain in achieving political objectives. It is unfortunate that U.S. military history had taught this lesson before and it was ignored. The Vietnam-era strategic hamlet policy was based off the British experience with a similar policy in Malaya, but failure to recognize the essential differences of the Vietnamese and Malayan environments doomed this policy. Language and cultural training must be institutionalized within PME curricula so that the Armed Forces can develop an appreciation of alternative perspectives and expand their understanding of the issues that may affect the achievement of strategic objectives. In addition to service schools, this type of training can be done within the community colleges and universities across the country. Incentivizing this training for both Active Component and Reserve Component members would be a cost effective means of ensuring the Armed Forces possess the resident knowledge to understand the complexities of the twenty-first century security environment.

Risk Assessment

As long as there is sufficient force structure built into the Active and Reserve Component endstrength to allow personnel to attend resident education without robbing combat units of leadership, there is no downside risk to this recommendation. All four areas of risk are mitigated by a more educated military. There is significant downside risk, however, in reducing force structure without educating the force that remains to be able to adapt to the diverse and complex threats of the future.

Recommendation Eight: Avoid a Strict Cost Benefit Analysis for Defense Planning

Throughout the twentieth century, civilian and military leadership have attempted to apply business model principles to increase military efficiency and cut the costs of national security. This approach has invariably led to tension between military and civilian leadership when the military fails to meet business model goals and has had disastrous effects when these goals did not match strategic objectives. The non-linearity of defense planning defies a business model approach: "war is inevitably tragic, inefficient, and uncertain, and it is important to be skeptical of systems analyses, computer models, game theories, or doctrines that suggest otherwise"[79]

As it applies to defense planning, efficiency can be thought of as the ability to accomplish a task with a minimum expenditure of time, effort and money. Effectiveness, on the other hand, should be thought of as producing the desired result. For the purposes of national security objectives, achieving the desired result is all that really matters.

The goal of any business model is to maximize profits. Despite, ample evidence to the contrary, business models assume the actors in the system will react rationally. That is, they look to maximize their utility from a given action. In order to accomplish this, redundancy and inefficiency must be eliminated. Redundancy in military affairs, however, is a virtue. It provides the flexibility to overcome friction and account for

---

[79] Gates, "A Balanced Strategy," 28.

unknown variables associated with confronting an animate, thinking adversary: it is also expensive and inefficient.[80] The business model approach, that ruthlessly seeks out this inefficiency, with the goal of eliminating it, erodes the military's capacity to overcome friction and unknown variables.

Civilian and military leadership should avoid the temptation of using business models because they "cannot be applied to the conduct of war; their basic purposes are so hugely different that they cannot be reconciled."[81] Instead of a business model approach, defense planner analyses should focus on those measures that decrease risk and increase the probability of success. Determining those measures of effectiveness can prove to be very challenging. The use of enemy body counts in Vietnam, which implied "efficiency" in military operations, provided no useful metric of effectiveness in the complex counterinsurgency environment where control of the population was the key to achieving objectives. Spending levels have been used as a measure of success in Iraq and Afghanistan, but they speak nothing about what services are being provided at the local level where objectives are actually achieved.

This is not to say that the military should not look for efficiencies in accomplishing objectives: reducing operating costs free up funds that can be used for additional training or invested into programs that preserve and enhance the force. The operational use of horses ended in the 1920's, yet British artillery units had a seventh man on their Table of Organization whose function was to hold the team's horses. It was not until an inspector

---

[80] Frederick W. Kagan, "A Dangerous Transformation. Donald Rumsfeld Means Business. That's a Problem", The Wall Street Journal, November 12, 2003, www.opinionjournal.com/extra/?id=110004289 (accessed 26 November, 2010)

[81] Milan Vego, "Is the Conduct of War a Business?" *Joint Forces Quarterly*, Issue 59, (4th Quarter 2010), 57.

witnessed the inefficiency that the seventh man's billet was converted into a more effective utilization of manpower. The military must be constantly looking for the proverbial seventh man and either eliminating or converting those billets.

The costs of national defense are high, but not nearly as high as fighting a war for which the nation has not prepared. Civilian and military leadership must accept the inefficiencies associated with redundancy as a cost of reducing risk and increasing the probability of success.

CHAPTER 4: CONCLUSION

In conclusion, the volatility, uncertainty, complexity and ambiguity of the strategic environment make it likely that the United States will maintain its perfect record of incorrectly predicting its next war. The key to effectiveness for near-to-mid term force planning is maintaining balance between conventional and irregular warfare capabilities with sufficient depth to provide the requisite flexibility to adapt when adversaries do not react as our forecasting models predict. This balanced force must remain capable of coping with either a general or limited war. The United States must always be capable of "fielding forces that are versatile and that, in aggregate, can undertake missions across the full range of plausible challenges."[1] The United States already has the best answer to the challenges it faces in place. An honest look at roles and missions, specifically the assignment of different competencies between the Active, and the Reserve Components provides the United States with the best solution to be able to meet current challenges, mitigate strategic surprise from traditional rivals, and provide strategic depth in the event of an emergency. Twentieth-century U.S. history provides lessons learned on how to balance the force.

Achieving this balance will require breaking the present-day paradigm regarding the roles and missions of the Active and Reserve Components. This effort will be more evolutionary than revolutionary. Fiscal restraints will require the military to rely more on the other elements of national power to accomplish national objectives, but the military

---

[1] U.S. Department of Defense, *Quadrennial Defense Review Report.* (Washington, DC: February 2010), 43.

will still have the responsibility to backstop those efforts should they fail. Savings from defense spending must be invested in the other forms of national power for U.S. policy to be effective. This may not result in the desired savings that many are hoping for. It is imperative, though, that Americans understand that security comes through a planned defense and not disarmament.

The recommendations in this paper are the author's attempt at solving the non-linear problem of fighting and preparing for war within the current fiscal constraints. These recommendations are based on the premise that "armies have always existed, first and foremost, to fight conventional wars," yet the demand for counterinsurgency and security and stability operations as well as nuclear deterrence requires that the military invest in those capabilities.[2] Further, the recommendations realize that "the U.S. cannot take its current [conventional] dominance for granted and needs to invest in the programs, platforms, and personnel that will ensure that dominance's persistence."[3] They attempt to mitigate the strategic risks the Nation faces, with the understanding that "however carefully we think about the future; however thorough our preparations; however coherent and thoughtful our concepts, training and doctrine; we will be surprised" and that they key to success will lie in the military's ability to adapt to that surprise.[4] The size of the Total Force is preserved while reducing personnel cost by approximately twenty percent. Roles and missions are rebalanced to address more effectively the

---

[2] Ian F.W. Becket, ed., The Roots of Counterinsurgency: Armies and Guerilla Warfare 1900-1945 (London: Blandford Press, 1988), 15.

[3] Robert M. Gates, "A Balanced Strategy: Reprogramming the Pentagon for a New Age," *DISAM Journal of International Security Assistance Management* (March 2009; 31, 1; Military Module), 13.

[4] U.S. Joint Forces Command, The Joint Operating Environment 2008: Challenges and Implications for the Future Joint Forces (Norfolk, VA: U.S. Joint Forces Command, 15 October 2008), 3.

diverse threats of the twenty-first century. The author believes these recommendations provide the best option for dealing with threats across the spectrum of conflict.

In many ways, the recommendations in this paper are not ideal solutions; resource constrained solutions seldom are. They will require hard choices and risk will have to be assumed in some areas. They will require significant force structure and cultural changes that will demand the total commitment by military and civilian leadership to overcome paradigmatic thinking and parochial biases. However, their purpose is to provide the United States with the strategic flexibility and agility to adapt its security responses to an uncertain world and avoid repeating the record of past American first battles while preserving the economic wellbeing of the Nation.

APPENDIX 1: ELEVEN COMMON STRATEGY SINS

1. Failure to recognize or take seriously the scarcity of resources

2. Mistaking strategic goals for strategy

3. Failure to recognize or state the strategic problem

4. Choosing poor or unattainable strategic goals

5. Not defining the strategic challenge competitively

6. Making false presumptions about one's own competence or the likely causal linkages between one's strategy and one's goals

7. Insufficient focus on strategy due to such things as trying to satisfy too many different stakeholders or bureaucratic processes

8. Inaccurately determining one's areas of comparative advantage relative to the opposition

9. Failure to realize that few individuals possess the cognitive skills and mindset to be competent strategists

10. Failure to understand the adversary[1]

11. Failure to understand ourselves[2]

---

[1] The ten "common strategy sins" as presented by Richard Rumelt in CSBA seminar, "Thoughts on Business Strategy," on Sept 25, 2007, cited by Andrew F. Krepinevich and Barry D. Watts in, *Regaining Strategic Competence: Strategy for the Long Haul* (Washington, DC: Center for Strategic and Budgetary Analysis, 2009), x.

[2] The eleventh sin as added by Walter McDougall, "Can the United States Do Grand Strategy?" *The Telegram* (April 2010) http://www.fpri.org/telegram/201004.mcdougall.usgrandstrategy.html.

BIBLIOGRAPHY

Beaufre, Andre. *An Introduction to Strategy.* New York: Frederick and Praeger, 1965.

Becket, Ian F. W. *The Roots of Counterinsurgency: Armies and Guerilla Warfare 1900-1945.* London: Blandford Press, 1988.

Bernado, C. Joseph, and Eugene H., Ph.D. Bacon. *American Military Policy Its Development Since 1775.* Harrisburg, PA: The Telegraph Press, 1961.

Binnendijk, Hans, and Stuart E., eds. Johnson. *Transforming for Stabilization and Reconstruction Operations.* Washington, DC: National Defense University Press, 2004.

Caldwell, Stephen. "Beyond the BUR: Why the Two-War Strategy Will Survive the Quadrennial Defnse Review." *Armed Forces Journal International 134, No. 8,* March 1997: 38-41.

Clausewitz, Carl Von. *On War.* Edited by Michael Howard and Peter Paret. Translated by Michael Howard and Peter Paret. New York, NY: Alfred A. Knopf, 1993.

Clawson, Patrick ed. *Strategic Assessment 1997 Flashpoints and Force Structure.* Washington, DC: National Defense University Institute for National Strategic Studies, 1997.

Cline, Ray S. *Washington Command Post: The Operations Division.* Washington, DC: U.S. Army Center of Military History, 1951.

Commission on the National Guard and Reserves. "Transforming the National Guard and Reserves Into a 21st Century Operational Force, Final Report to Congress and Secretary of Defense." Arlington, VA, January 31, 2008.

Congressional Budget Office. *Long Term Implications of the FY10 Defense Budget.* Washington, DC: Congressional Budget Office, January 2010.

Cordesman, Anthony H. *US Defense Planning: Creating Reality Based Strategy, Planning, Programming, and Budgeting.* Washington, DC: Center for Strategic and International Studies, July 2010.

Council, National Security. "Report to the President Pursuant to the President's Directive of January 31, 1950." NSC-68, Washington, D.C., 1950.

Cronin, Patrick M. *Restraint: Recalibrating American Strategy.* Washington, DC: Center For A New American Security, June 2008.

Davis, Thomas. "2 MRC or Not 2 MRC: The Bottom Up Review's Two-Conflict Force-Sizing Criteria Has Served the Nation Well." *Armed Forces Journal International 134, No. 6,* January 1997: 46-47.

Donovan, Robert J. *Conflict and Crisis, The Presidency of Harry S. Truman, 1945-1948.* New York: WW Norton and Company, 1977.

Eaglen, Mackenzie. "Backgrounder, No. 2418, U.S. Defense Spending: The Mismatch Between Plans and Resources." *The Heritage Foundation.* 7 June 2010. http://www.report.heritage.org/bg2418 (accessed July 1, 2010).

Edwards, Paul M. *To Acknowledge a War: The Korean War in American Memory.* Westport, CT: Greenwood Press, 2000.

Fautua, David t. ""Long Pull" Army: NSC-68, the Korean War and the Creation of the Cold War Army." *Journal of Military History 61, No. 1*, January 1997: 93-120.

Flournoy, Michele A. "Twelve Strategy Decisions for the Next Administrations." In *Strategy and Force Planning, Fourth Edition*, by Strategy and Forces Faculty ed. Security, 34-36. Newport, RI: Naval War College Press, 2004.

Gates, Robert M. "A Balanced Strategy: Reprogramming the Pentagon for a New Age." *Foreign Affairs* 88, no. 1 (Jan/Feb 2009): 28-40.

Gizewski, Peter J. "Army 2040: The Global Security Environment: Emerging Trends and Potential Challenges." *Paper prepared for the Annual Meeting of the Canadian Political Science Association, Carleton University.* Ottawa, 27 May 2009.

Government Accountability Office. *GAO-07-828, Military Personnel: DOD Needs to Establish a Strategy and Improve Transparency Over Reserve and National Guard Compensation to Manage Significant Growth in Cost.* Washington, DC: Govenrment Printing Office, January 31, 2008.

Government Accountability Office. *GAO-09-989, Reserve Forces Army Needs to Finalize Implementation Plan and Funding Strategy for Sustaining an Operational Reserve.* Washington, DC: Government Prinitng Office, September 2009.

Grimmett, Richard F. *Instances of Use of United States Armed Forces Abroad, 1798-2009.* washington, D.C.: Congressional Research Service, 2010.

Hammes, Thomas X. *The Sling and The Stone: On War in the 21st Century.* St. Paul, MN: Zenith Press, 2004.

Harrison, Todd. *Analysis of the FY 2010 Defense Budget Request.* Washington, DC: Center for Strategic and Budgetary Assessments, 2010.

Heller, Charles E. *The New Military Strategy and Its Impact on the Reserve Components.* Thesis, Carlisle, PA: Strategic Studies Institute, US Army War College, 1991.

Johnson, David E. "From Frontier Constabulary to Modern Army." In *The Challenge of Change: Military Institutions and New Realities, 1918-1941*, by Harold R. Winton and David R. Mets. Lincoln, NE: University of Nebraska Press, 2000.

Kagan, Frederick W. "A Dangerous Transformation. Donald Rumsfeld Means Business. That's a Problem." *The Wall Street Journal, Opinion Journal.* November 12, 2003. http://www.opinionjournal.com/extra/?id=110004289 (accessed November 26, 2010).

Kennedy, Paul. *The Rise and Fall of the Great Powers.* New York: Random House, 1987.

Krepinevich, Andrew F., and Barry D. Watts. *Regaining Strategic Competence: Strategy for the Long Haul.* Washington, DC: Center for Strategic and Budgetary Analysis, 2009.

Krulak, Charles C. "Enduring Instrument: The Force in Readiness in National Defense." *Strategic Review XXV, No. 2*, Spring 1997: 7-12.

Lacquement, Richard A. *The American Interest.* September-October 2010. http://the-american-interest.com/article.cfm?piece=860 (accessed October 1, 2010).

McDougall, Walter A. "Can the United States Do Grand Strategy?" *The Telegram*, April 2010: http://www.fpri.org/telegram/201004.mcdougall.usgrandstrategy.html.

MelNyk, Les'. *Mobilizing for the Storm: The Army National Guard in Operations DESERT SHIELD and STORM.* National Guard Bureau Office of Public Affairs Historical Services Division, 2001.

Moskin, J. Robert. *The U.S. Marine Corps Story, Third Revised Edition.* Boston: Little, Brown and Company, 1992.

Nagl, John A., and Travis Sharp. "Operational For What? The Future of the Guard and Reserves." *Joint Forces Quarterly, Issue 59*, 4th Quarter 2010.

Nagl, John, and Travis Sharp. *An Indispensible Force: Investing in America's National Guard and Reserves.* Washington, D.C.: Center For New American Security, 2010.

Nolan, Janne, and Mark Strauss. "Rogue's Gallery." *Brown Journal of World Affairs 4, No. 1*, Winter 1997 - Spring 1998: 21-38.

Perry, William J. "Defense in an Age of Hope." *Foreign Affairs 75, No. 6*, November 1996 - December 1996: 64-78.

Perry, William J. "Preventative Defense." *Foreign Affairs 75, No.6*, November 1996 - December 1996: 64-79.

Project on National Security Reform. *Forging a New Shield.* Arlington, VA: Center for the Study of the Presidency, November 2008.

Rearden, Stephen L. "Reassessing the Gaither Report's Role." *Diplomatic History Vol 25, No. 1*, Winter 2001.

Record, Jeffrey. *The Creeping Irrelevance of U.S. Force Planning.* Carlisle Barracks, PA: Strategic Studies Institute, 1998.

Robb, Charles S. "rebuilding a Concensus on Defense." *Parameters 26, No. 4*, Winter 1996 - Winter 1997: 4-12.

Romjue, John L. *From Active Defense to AirLand Battle: The Development of Army Doctrine, 1973-1982.* Fort Monroe, VA: Historical Office, U.S. Army Training and Doctrine Command, 1984.

Shalikashvili, John M. "United States Armed Forces: A Prospectus." *Vital Speeches of the Day LXIII, No. 6*, January 1997: 165-168.

Stellini, Edward. "Force Structure Planning Considerations." *Air University Review*, May-June 1971: http://www.aipower.au.af.mil/airchronicles/aureview/1971/may-jun/Stellini.html.

Tarr, David W. *American Security in the Nuclear Age.* New York: Macmillan Publishing Company, 1966.

U.S. Army Center of Military History. "American Military History, Volume 2." *U.S. Army Center of Military History.* http://www.history.army.mil/books/amh-v2/amh%20v2 (accessed November 13, 2010).

U.S. Congress. House of Representatives. House Amred Services Committee. "The 2010 Quadrennial Defense Review." *H.A.S.C. 111-122.* Washington, DC: 111th Cong., 2nd sess., February 4, 2010.

U.S. Department of Defense. "Department of Defense Directive 3000.07, Irregular Warfare (IW)." Washington, DC, December 1, 2008.

—. "Department of Defense Instruction 1235.12, Accessing the Reserve Components (RC)." Washington, DC, 4 February 2010.

—. "Department of Defense Instruction 3000.05, Stbility Operations." Washington, DC, September 16, 2009.

—. "Force Application Functional Concept." Washington, DC, 5 March 2004.

—. "National Defense Strategy." Washington, DC, June 2008.

—. *Quadrennial Defense Review.* Washington: Government Printing Office, 2010.

U.S. Department of the Army. "The Army Almanac." Washington, D.C., 1950.

U.S. Department of War. "Report of the Secretary of War to the President." 1922.

U.S. Joint Forces Command. "The Joint Operating Environment 2008: Challenges and Implications for the Future Joint Forces." Norfolk, VA: U.S. Joint Forces Command, 15 October 2008.

U.S. National Security Council. "National Security Council Document 68." Washington, DC, April 7, 1950.

U.S. President. "Guard and Reserves Define Spirit of America." *Remarks by the President of the United States to Employees at the Pentagon.* http://www.whitehouse.gov/news/releases/2001/09/20010917-3.html, September 17, 2001.

—. "National Security Strategy." Washington, DC, 2010.

U.S. War Office. *Report of the Secretary of War to the President, 1933.* Washington, DC: Government Printing Office, 1933.

United States. "Kellogg-Briand Pact." *League of Nations Treaty Series, Volume 94.* August 27, 1928.

Vego, Milan. "Is the Conduct of War a Business?" *Joint Forces Quarterly*, 4th Quarter, 2010: 57-65.

White, John. "US Marine Corps Force Structure: Another Look." Thesis.

Winkler, John D. "Developing an Operational Reserve: A Policy and Historical Context and the Way Forward." *Joint Forces Quarterly Issue 59*, 4th Quarter 2010: 14-20.